# THE GLORY OF RAINBOW

## UNIQUE COLLECTIONS OF POEMS OF TZAR QUETZALCOATL

TZAR QUETZALCOATL AYUSH SINGH

ISBN 979-888521982-2

‘wanna dedicate this book to the special friend of mine who encouraged me to write more and more, she was the one who helped me to write the first rhyming stanza of my first poem. Really thankful to my English Teacher who was the one to help me out and praise me for my first two poems. ‘twas genetic so want to thank my maternal grandfather who was also having a great quality of writing small rhyming poems, and this DEDICATION will be a motivating force for my DEDICATION towards writing…..

# Contents

# Contents

# Foreword

The first poet and writer I observed in my life was a friend of mine, who was not more than 15 years of age, then. The most considerable thing I noticed in him was his love for humanity and realization of each sentiment. No matter whose pain it was, it would surely affect him and I feel that's the most important factor you need to become a good Author.

Proceeding in his life endeavours, he started jotting down his emotions and creating a garland of words and sentiments. No matter what type and age you are now but you would have gone through the age of "teenage ". The book " The Glory of Rainbow " is a sum-up of approximately all the feelings and thoughts a teenager ever goes through. I, personally, find each poem of the author relatable and is always keen to read from him a little more. Not only the sentiments but the vocabulary and library devices in this book are also of great knowledge, adding more joy to the reader's heart. This book would be my suggestion to all the curious readers.

Shivanshi Singh

Blogger

# Preface

**The Glory of Rainbow** is not merely a book having constellated poetries, it is splattered ink page with lots of emotions and true mirrored feelings of mine. The main motive to publish this piece is to spread the vibrancy in the life of my readers like the rainbow spreads its pulchritudinous beauty in the blue blanket.

Having assumed that I have to live my life happily, I have withheld myself from the taunts of society and doesn't care what the people around me are poking to make me feel down. In the age of exploration, I'm confused with different emotions and genders, and this book expresses all of it my success and my downfalls.

This book consists of more than half of my poetry, and each poem will give you the knowledge of something or the other, whether about the literary devices or about the different textures of vocabulary. The poem in itself is a social solution for a secular society, and yes the alliterations you are going to mingle with them a lot.

***"If they get harsh, be resilient enough to heal their harshness."*** is what I try to do, even if you are in pain try to heal not with revenge not with the feeling of enmity but with the healing power of meditating love.

# Acknowledgements

***"Devise thyself for the abysmal situation at the best hour."*** and at this pious hour want my readers to feel my love for them, and the true heart of mine throbs for them always. Thankful to my parents for giving me birth and the one reading this for adding up one more.

# Prologue

This book surrounds around the Emotions and Feelins a newbie teen writer, and he is the only main protagonist of this book, and he is none other than the Author of the book, whose social perspective and eagerness to change the world has penned pulchritudinous pieces.

# 1. Star of Night

*The days have light ,*
*and night have dullness .*
*The students who are bright ,*
*don't sit useless .*
*They WORK , WORK , WORK ,*
*day and night ,*
*and shine like a star bright in night .*
*Be one of them and be bright like a star ,*
*throughout your life each and every hour .*
*With good memories in your mind ,*
*being gentle and kind .*
*Passing all the difficulties in your way ,*
*by not remembering the days which have passed away .*
*Knowing the truth of all mysteries ,*
*getting the knowledge of all histories .*
*Being one of the bright student ,*
*by not showing prudents .*
*As it will lead them to disaster ,*
*and will take their all laughter .*
*Be a star bright night ,*
*always shining in night .*

# 2. Heart of Motherland

*Life is so precious*
*We should live it with full of joy and happiness*
*By not being rumpus all around*
*Its a human nature*
*To be robust and orthodox*
*He wastes his all time oscillating around*
*Notorious humans have nothing to do*
*They create a nuinsance all around*
*He has a louche infront of others*
*As he do not know locution for others*
*They way of his speaking matters a lot*
*Infront of others in each and every lot*
*He cannot leviate like birds*
*But his ambitions leviate*
*He deviates from his job*
*By being a boa then and now*
*O' humans be like Jesus and all*
*By not creating a noise at all*
*It is a soft heart of your motherland*
*Keep it safe in your hand*

# 3. The tenderness of being Far Away

*The tenderness of being faraway*
*Reminds me of passing days*
*Which is enjoyed by me with my loved ones*
*But days are passing outrun*
*But now I feel bit scared for my future*
*That am I abducting my dreams*
*Or am I creating new ways deem*
*Now remembering that how far I reached on the way of life*
*I should not weary for upcoming days*
*I should welcome the gifted life*
*Lets have courage to meet the upcoming barriers*
*They are like episodes which ends after another*
*As the people will encourage us to move on*
*Towards our goal on each morn*
*Lets not mourn on being far away*
*But should merry for one step we reached today..*

# 4. If words had fragrance

*If words had fragrance*
*Then people would found it abhorrent*
*As they'll found it astonishing*
*How can their words have a smell*
*Their words would tell about them*
*About their personalities in every realm*
*Their words would describe them better than anyone else*
*Which may lead them to criminalize*
*If words had fragrance*
*They would better explain feeling of lover*
*In the hall of perfumes to odour*
*They would better explain the sadness of a philospher*
*In each morn and eve to adhere*
*But there are no possibilities for fragrance*
*As it is an imagination and has no appearance*
*So be chill as you wont be criminalize*
*Be happy and dont socialize*

# 5. Mom

*I never thought I would be like this*
*I only thoght for a gentle bliss*
*When i see roses in my garden*
*It gives me bliss and a pardon*
*It gives me care and propine*
*For you are bit of mine*
*I was never like this.....for your gentle bliss*
*I am bless to have you and ofcourse your kiss*
*You gave me your life, you words as a clip*
*I never thought I would be like this*
*I gently remember those days of you and mine*
*When I was a churl of a mine*
*With your love you accepted me and gave me a life*
*Today I stand by you*
*I never thoght i would be like this*
*You gave me love*
*Which is worn as care*
*And a morn and eve and my life*
*I will respect you throghout my life*
*Love you mom*

# 6. To love Someone

*when we love someone*
*we are in abrasion*
*we only love someone*
*but the other one is totally no one*
*is this a love to love someone*
*or it is just and adulation*
*to love someone does not means to give everything*
*its just an attraction to a new being*
*a being who is known to us for a day and month*
*breaks our heart, shatters our mind when he is done*
*its just an infatuation*
*we should make our love our adoration*
*without any alienation*
*as we only love someone for care*
*and in return we should get abundant to share*
*this happens when we love someone out of care*

# 7. Take me to the place

*Take me to the place out of debonair*
*where there is only nature and virtual affair*
*take me to the place where*
*I can found love without despair*
*Is there any place for me out there?*
*where I can cry without comply*
*because I want to live my life with no despair*
*my mother nature always call me with care*
*but due to my lithargic act it is no worth to be there*
*Is there any place for me out there?*
*where I can share my problems without fear*
*where I can lay down with full of care*
*and share my problems with the person who is present there*
*Is there any place for me out there?*
*where im alone with my personal affair*
*so that I can breathe fresh air*
*and work on my weaknesses with no regrets and fear*
*so that Im ready and aware*
*aware of things which are going to begin*
*Is there any place where I can found peace and unity with no despair?*
*I am sure i will found that place one day out of fear*

# 8. Curse to be black

*They called me black,*
*For me it was an awful attack .*
*They figured my complexion as my abnormality,*
*but it was their verbal brutality.*
*They wanted to make fun of me,*
*as they believed themselves to be bourgeoisie.*
*I wasn't their helot but they treated me like that,*
*they thought i was like a tongue - tied gnat.*
*But now its time for me to rise up,*
*its time for building up my intensities and to rise from this hyssop.*
*I want my rights and this is a cheer of my pride,*
*I'm making this heartfull allure worldwide.*
*Being black is not a curse,*
*none of you can return my regality in reimburse.*
*You are deriding of me because of my dark skin,*
*this is an ignominy and a infelicious sin.*
*They call me black,*
*as they have no locutions to collate me with a slack.*
*but they are unaware that a small slack has a hefty heat inside,*
*which is so sturdy that it can break this curse of racism worldwide.*

# 9. Feeling Low

*Whenever I feel squat or truncated,*
*around me a discrete abode is acclimated.*
*But I know if I pursue this prostration,*
*I will disburse my entire entity in accusation .*
*Remember one thing feeling stubby is not an emulsion for everything,*
*you should not lessen your aspirations and credence.*
*Detach all the commodities which are abducting,*
*and you should start perceiving your impedance.*
*Start gaining the grips where you shortfall,*
*rather than being its butterball.*
*You should get the better of all your blunders,*
*and should begin your hard work to burst like thunders.*
*Remember one thing that nothing is gain without paying,*
*so work out with dedication day and night.*
*You should fight with your full strength from the upcoming graying ,*
*keep your dedication, credence and aspirations alive by being forthright.*

# 10. Seasons vs People

*People around us are like seasons ,*
*as they fall in our being with some reasons.*
*As seasons are changed periodically ,*
*these individuals enter into our life methodically.*
*Seasons create a tranquil surrounding,*
*in which people have pleasure in abounding.*
*Seasons are varying and beautiful,*
*they fill our life with triumph and make it mirthful.*
*Preluding with the first the hot summer,*
*people seems to be bursting in it with anger.*
*The autumn is so shrivelled and mild ,*
*most of the parents linger at home to play with their child.*
*Soon invades the warm and balmy monsoon ,*
*people of different ages love to have fritters in rainy moon.*
*Then comes up freezing and numbing winters,*
*people desire to snug themselves and keenly hold back for blistering summers .*

# 11. Whenever I write for my Country

*Whenever I write for my Country ,*
*I'm thronged with lot of gallantry.*
*My country has hundreds of torrents and chiliad of burgs,*
*Its beauty is adorable and also has number of cirques.*
*Whenever I write for my Country ,*
*There is no pique and abhorrence in my entity .*
*My country has most voguish democracy ,*
*Its intent is to meet its denizens adequacy.*

*Whenever I write for my Nation ,*
*I pen for it without any deterrent.*
*My Nation always succours the one who is in destitution ,*
*It endeavours to eradicate its natives predicament.*
*Whenever I write for my Nation,*
*I must divulge that it has no aggression .*
*My Nation has always helped its vicinal sovereign states,*
*It always proselytized amity and asked every man to venerate their authentic race .*
*Whenever I write for my Motherland ,*
*I dwam to end my course of life on its strand.*
*I'm proud to be my country's citizen ,*
*As I'm blessed to have India as my Country and I am its acknowledged*

*citizen.*

# 12. I feel I don't exist

*I feel I don't exist*
*when someone shatters my heart*
*I feel I don't exist*
*when I am all deserted*
*This feeling of non - existence*
*is deterorating my entire entity*
*But is it normal to have such vhemences ?*
*Or it is just a mere grief?*
*It is my heartfull allure that*
*never existed!*
*Not to cry or have pain*
*for the one whose presence*
*never lasted.*

# 13. Teachers are roots and we are fruits

*Teachers are momentous gift from god ,*
*we are like a grass and they are our sod .*
*Teachers are library of knowledge,*
*they give us enlightenment without any begrudges.*
*Teachers edify us with lot of warmth and affection ,*
*they furbish our comprehension so that we are moulded with perfection.*
*Teachers are like our parents,*
*we share our thoughts and predicaments with them without any abatements.*
*Teachers are with us throughout our life ,*
*they guide us with integrity and incentivize us as they have become a joyous part of our life.*
*A big thank you to all the teachers who have irradiated the lamp of knowledge,*
*"Teachers are roots and we are fruits" this will always encourage.*

# 14. YOUR QUESTION : MY ANSWER

*Something is destroying the sacredness of this world ,*
*I fear that what will happen if in few decades our mother will become a netherworld .*
*Our mother has seen many rulers and many colonisers ,*
*Who have loved and judged her people out of hatred and kindness .*
*But this cheer and joy that we are celebrating today seems to be declining ,*
*Our violence has troubled our mother to lose her fining .*

*You enjoy oneness but you fight on the borders with rage ,*
*Your hatred , jealousy , enimity has now blended with courage .*

*Our virtuous mother has taught you how to be peaceful ,*
*But nothing makes you care and you are asking me how to be peaceful ?*
*Ask yourself are you right if you are fighting a war by being violent ,*
*You will find your answer to your question 'how to be peaceful?' in a sight .*

# 15. Corruption mingled with Pollution

*Pollution , Corruption and Adulteration you have a dusty robe ,*
*let's find a solution before you make us impecunious .*
*Do not dare to mingle your ineptness with my pious soul ,*
*You won't be accepted by us till time you are a corrupted soul .*
*Pollution , Corruption and Adulteration you have a dusty robe ,*
*let's find a solution before you make us impecunious .*
*Snollygosters think they are sharp,*
*they have started welcoming you without knowing your bastardized stamp.*
*Pollution , Corruption and Adulteration you have a dusty robe ,*
*let's find a solution before you make us impecunious .*
*Cruel humans cheat to hide their terminological inexactitudes ,*
*they have fear and regret as they are not superior to welcome you with your murky attitude .*
*Pollution , Corruption and Adulteration you have a dusty robe ,*
*let's be aware of your wicked nature so that we can gift our Mother Earth a clean and pure shining robe .*

# 16. Birthday Month : Month to remember

*You came like a boon for me to remember ,*
*My family sat near the fire watching its each ember.*
*Suddenly they heard a cry and they smiled ,*
*It was just a new born baby who cried .*
*Everyone was excited that it was boy and they were in glee ,*
*When they started staring in the window of the room they found that the child who cried was me.*

# 17. An elegy of a Mongrel

*She entered the world of humans when she was six ,*
*when she was surrounded by us in cliques.*
*She was strange to us and we named the mongrel beautifully ,*
*Her goodness and fate can not be explained in this elegy .*
*The mongrel was brave enough and was tough ,*
*soon in her body and voice she brought gruff .*
*Nothing more she had to gain and to possess ,*
*it was just her goodness , just her goodness , just her goodness .*
*Today she is helpless and lying in dust ,*
*after giving birth to six pups now she is in disgust .*
*Her life ended on the note of bravery ,*
*but selfish humans are still sunk in bribery .*
*Mongrel entered our world and established a beautiful bond ,*
*but she was unaware of the hatred she will get when she will pass on .*

# 18. A kiss to the beauty of Earth

*You are so beautiful Oh my Earth ,*
*Holding bravely different worlds with love .*
*Worlds of different traditions and different culture ,*
*Symbolises the love that we possess*
*for one another .*
*Oh Earth your beauty is turning spotted ,*
*As to all your care and protections are trotted .*
*The months have gone and years have passed ,*
*but no gift is awarded to protect your garls .*
*We celebrate festivals with you in mirth ,*
*As we are the only sensible ones whom*
*you've given birth .*
*Today I want to kiss the beauty of*
*my mother whom I've always loved,*
*She is not only for usage and*
*beautification she is our precious mother*
*Earth .*

# 19. Couplets of Spring ( Vasant Panchami )

*The time when flowers bloom*
*enjoying the calmness of wind,*
*Its the time when nature kisses*
*its beauty and is determined .*
*There is chaos in the market where*
*vendors are shouting on top of their voices ,*
*Selling and buying the precious idol*
*and yellow rag with warmth .*
*There is happiness and mirth on each face,*
*Its the time to welcome the epitome*
*of knowledge, before the $40^{th}$ day of spring is there.*
*Bells are ringing in temples, its the*
*indication of the warm affection ,*
*Instruments are being soothly played*
*to welcome the mother .*
*She is the mother of knowledge , arts*
*and music and is called by many names*
*commonly 'Maa Saraswati',*
*Today all worship her to show respect*
*to her peaceful preachings of music and divinity .*

# 20. Your Touch

*Your fingers try to touch me from beneath ,*
*as your intent is to invade me from underneath .*
*I feel safe with you and my intents are strong for you ,*
*but a question prompts up , your touch isn't telling that good of you .*
*I'm clear to my thoughts and I do not wish to tangle with them ,*
*sometimes you make me feel so insecure that I have to tell my parents I can't live alone without them .*
*Your fingers are gentle in public and vicious in lone ,*
*Your touch turns to stripping when you find me alone .*
*I fear to speak the words for you as they shake through my tongue ,*
*I do not wish to have that unwanted devil touch from your tongue .*

# 21. Shhh it's not right

*Shhh, it's not right,*
*don't feel my body*
*your psyche may go up in smoke*
*dare not to hold me tight.*
*Shhh, it's not right,*
*kisses on neck and*
*red marks on my collarbone,*
*you were a monster that night.*
*Shhh, it's not right,*
*every time you break me*
*break me hard so that I can not console,*
*So, silly things prove your might.*
*Shhh, it's not right,*
*I cry making my surroundings wet,*
*still, you don't fear as you have to prove your grit.*
*I cry in pain sweating and screaming telling you*
*' Shhh it's not right '*

# 22. Tranquility of Emotions

*Emotions are dead because the body isn't responding,*
*it's all the illusionary thoughts that are gatecrashing.*
*It's hard to be happy and easy to be sad,*
*sadness succor itself when the day is bad.*
*None to complain as the time goes vain,*
*hardly something is sensed because the body had turned itself to a drain.*
*Happiness seems to be the queen of felicity,*
*she explores lots of fun and joy fullness with little creativity.*
*It's a burning minister Anger quenching one's thirst and is extremely filthy,*
*wasted expenses and resulting poverty which is major treachery.*
*Why so? is questioned because sadness has turned itself to the airy layer,*
*the King that covers my emotions but still, the tranquility lies somewhere far away.*

# 23. The Devil's Beauty

*It was twirling in the rain,*
*bathing in the heart alluring shower.*
*It seemed to be in utter fain,*
*It strewed the emerald beauty that enchanted it.*
*It was dancing being insane!*
*Being insane! what a triggering fact!*
*it wasn't a human but a Pothos.*
*who felt the breeze blowing with the spirit of love,*
*when each drop touched its greenery it shoved.*
*The sky was having a fondness for the twig,*
*but no motion inside the Devil's ivy was spotted.*
*The clinging plant was admiring for something else,*
*Yes! it was waiting for the drizzle to come and blend with its breath.*
*Yes, the devil's breath!*
*The enchantress showed the magic,*
*sprinkled the virescent rays from it's clingy wand.*
*My eyes were flabbergasted when I had the*
*vision of true the beauty of the two natural fellows,*
*As I was captured by the Devil's beauty.*
*Yes, the Devil's beauty!*

# 24. The Incessant Thoughts

*Endless imaginations were transfixed*
*with the airy thoughts,*
*I was entering in gloominess as I*
*knew that my love was abstract.*
*My intellect was smitten to my agonies,*
*I denied the proposals as I already*
*possessed adamant worries.*
*Colossally afflicted, all the interpretations*
*turned out murky.*
*I gathered some courage but it was late,*
*I wasn't destined to cry but I marked it to my fate.*
*I had a penchant for some faded memories,*
*Memories that gave birth to pangs and miseries.*
*My hopes were alive but they were sophisticated*
*and warily.*
*They're still alive and my heart still strives.*

# 25. The Call

*Feeling the freezing flames of fumes,*
*the obvious old love of dunes.*
*I was sitting beside my bed jotting down*
*each moment,*
*I was waiting for a call of my ailment.*
*The twilight ushered with its melody,*
*My heart called me to live with ecstasy.*
*The beating life inside my chest was*
*fooled by philanderer,*
*The empyrean calls were rejected by my*
*inner whippersnapper.*
*I tried hard but failed almost every time,*
*fighting with the woe was another crime.*
*Still, there is a struggle of life,*
*which is as sharp as slaughterman's knife.*
*The call gets missed,*
*whenever I try to pamper myself with a kiss.*
*It can be only received,*
*when the misery of the heart is relieved.*

# 26. Why so? It is perishing

*Why such thoughts?*
*dimming the sparking light.*
*Why all taunts?*
*demising my emotional plight.*
*I cry on a soft bed,*
*but no one gives a damn to it.*
*Feeling lost on the deathbed,*
*nobody cares to feed me.*
*Why such emotions?*
*making the soul perish,*
*Why such thoughts?*
*making my spirit perish.*
*Lost lamenting,*
*feeling no way to escape.*
*all day the body is screaming,*
*the relationships broken, emotions are*
*cracked to cure them can I get any tape?*

# 27. The Child bears all

*The Child bears all,*
*cries and weeps.*
*He finds himself in creeps,*
*when there is a sudden fall.*
*The Child bears all*
*when passes childhood.*
*Struggles in adulthood,*
*'He' waits for his fairy doll.*
*The Child bears all,*
*the struggles of exam and broken*
*relationships are wain.*
*He experiences thousands of pains,*
*wishes to have his family after all.*
*Why a Child bears all?*
*isn't that silly to blame,*
*isn't society's concerns lame,*
*the child becomes lonely after all.*
*The Child bears all,*
*his tale can't be summarized.*
*His struggle isn't that concise,*
*striving hard he finally manages all the downfalls.*
*So you can't say that a child doesn't bears all!*

# 28. As I am going away from you

*As I am going away from you,*
*my mourning soul is shouting & screaming.*
*Perhaps your emotions are standstill and faded,*
*I know your hidden tears are bidding me adieu.*
*My glassy heart is annihilated,*
*I can feel the desertification of our bond.*
*It is very tough to erase the memories,*
*But it is a fact that society won't accept our bond.*
*Apart from relations, my peace of mind is shattered.*
*my speeches turned out murky, letters were faded*
*pulses were stopped, eyes were withdrawn,*
*when your winsome breath touched my soul my heart was flattered.*
*I find my emotions as floccinaucinihilipilification.*
*it's hard to forget your presence,*
*As I'm going away from you,*
*Don't feel stumbled, I may not speak or write,*
*but one day they'll accept us and I will return to your life.*

# 29. I will be Strong

*I dream to be strong,*
*My inner soul throngs.*
*heavy pulses dominate,*
*I shine, shake and stumble,*
*but I dream to be strong.*
*I limit my days to bring changes.*
*I decide to gain fame with no grudges,*
*but perhaps it turns out to be*
*the end of game.*
*Reminding myself what I'm struggling for?*
*I affirm myself to be strong.*
*Sad emotions pass by - anger is subdued,*
*Love is shallow and hate is high,*
*When there are mood swings I feel to cry.*
*but still I have feelings to be strong ,*
*as these sympathizing subfusc*
*sorrows won't last long.*

# 30. Life's Crucial Stage

*A crucial stage of life, am I the only one dreaming high?*
*The bells of the school, and tears of the joy,*
*was the unheard tale for the few.*
*Known to the fact that life isn't actualized,*
*barefooted emotions are subdued.*
*Just to know why it has been the crucial stage of life?*
*the soul lacks in clearing all of its dues.*
*The solutions to the worries are tuned with hate,*
*life is full of hurdles which include this crucial stage.*
*The sudden downfall of emotions is another factor of pain,*
*the hugging desires of humans are always quenched with pain.*
*Wishing to defenestrate the emotions there isn't outrage,*
*Well, it's not defined what's the unit to measure the pain,*
*it can not be declined as still there is a hopeful positive ray.*
*All of a sudden how the things change from words to bed,*
*of a sudden, it is shattered when you're mundane.*
*Thousands wish to cry and the cause is the same,*
*shattered soul is never satisfied as life is never the same.*
*Fooling around with physical desires one tries to gain fame,*
*and the time when he suffers understands*
*that crucial stage of life isn't the same.*

# 31. Imbalanced Emotions

*Shattering like crystals,*
*when touched the base of the soul.*
*Whenever there is a disturbance,*
*the eyes shed precious crystals.*
*Cluttered, casting, cults shine*
*and surmounts the beauty arose.*
*Ever since clutched with emotional stress*
*the fable to maintain the balance :*
*Not possible for this soul.*
*Withdrawn from the emotions,*
*the soul puts up its distressed piece.*
*To narrate what's the truth,*
*the law shambles underneath.*
*How daring these imbalances are?*
*None to amplify the ample or all.*
*How daring these emotions are?*
*To which sigh they lie is a mystery after all.*

# 32. Vague

*Pillows are drenched,*
*The heart isn't quenched.*
*Vague thoughts circling the entity*
*reminds me how much I've lost,*
*how much I've invested in upbringing these thoughts.*
*Watered willows are a wonderland, I'm trying to visit.*
*Feeling dull and delighted are my life's requisites.*
*Alas! I couldn't frame the things as I wanted,*
*I wasn't able to feel the things as I was vaguely exhausted.*
*Still, I want to visit the best place,*
*where I can enjoy the leftover part of mine.*
*Where I can enjoy the leftover part of mine.*
*Where I won't feel worried or troubled*
*I curiously want to cure my bruises,*
*which makes my heart suffer.*
*'Fuselage' isn't what we term ourselves*
*when our body is demolished,*
*Isn't that painful, helful, and dreadful?*
*I'm waiting for the second chance,*
*Even though I would be titled at last with the same.*
*Huh! Aren't we living with stuffed emotions?*
*Like the dumplings filled with veggies.*
*They use to taste tasty,*
*and we make ourselves feel nasty.*

*At last, what happens is -*
*Pillows are drenched,*
*The heart isn't quenched.*
*Vague thoughts circling the entity*
*reminds me how much I've lost,*
*how much I've invested in upbringing these thoughts.*

# 33. HE and HIS desires

*More than a hundred kilometers Cloud travels,*
*filled with ashes, smoke, and some of the human's bribes they love to handle.*
*HE writes the history of it and anonymously make it dirty,*
*without caring about it, HE makes himself a part of an underground mystery.*
*HE isn't concerned about it, HE doesn't feel empathetic to it,*
*Knowing its consequences HE doesn't want to improve some of it.*
*Yes, the Climate Issue, the Pollution, the Corruption,*
*HE knows it HE doesn't want it, yet HE is not going to change it.*
*It depends upon the faulty decisions of HIM,*
*as HE is the only one responsible for the deterioration of the environment.*
*Tons of flesh into HIS belly,*
*undressing Flora and Fauna makes HIM jolly.*
*What a disastrous sin HE is abiding HIMSELF to?*
*Shockingly HE won't be spared by the spontaneous effects of these tribulations.*
*You see my dear friend, how cruelly HE chops off those horns,*
*HE opens farms and factories - sells marine of this beautiful round with no fame expressions.*
*Still, HE wants HIMSELF to be called majesty by others: probably an unwanted truth.*
*Deterioration of Climate soothes HIM and still, HE gets warmth from this blanket.*

*Just apologies to my Mother who's flat land has raised such a sinner.*
*Abducting all laws and rules HE just wants to ruin HIS mother.*
*I will stand on the peak of this flat just for myu Mother's love,*
*Won't let HIM destroy this holy kingdom as HE is worling for disasters*
*and I for this land's love.*

# 34. Floating Cotton in the Blue Pond

*Supercalifragilisticexpialidocious Cumulus,*
*are you the only fluffy one whose brother is Nimbus.*
*So, you might inquire Stratus why it's dull,*
*I'm at a war with the soft Flannel remarked the state minister.*
*The pond in a straight shout screamed,*
*Are you fighting for a loftiest cotton-like cloud?*
*The blue pond was angry as Fractus occupied*
*all the mass she had!*
*Stratus was dull and was floating all around.*
*The Nimbus turned out to be quisling,*
*Blue Pond was saddened and doubted her parenting.*
*Crowning ceremony of Cumulus was well conducted,*
*As the result of it both the cotton Cumulus and Stratus were mated.*
*The pond was filled with hope and joy,*
*As she thought Cumulus and Stratus will handover a baby boy.*
*The fate turned opposite and was against the will of the pond,*
*when Stratus was aborted due to Nimbus treachery in abhor.*
*Fractus a doofus brat, collided with Nimbus*
*both together usurped the holy Cumulus*
*The curse of Stratus devastated the Fractonimbus reign*
*the Blue Pond wasn't able to bear the pain,*
*soon this resulted torrential rain.*

*The Pond's dusky robe was washed with merciful blessings of God.*
*the tale of Nimbus's Treachery was decietful of all*
*the couple were blessed by neonate named Stratocumulus.*
*The Pond became happy kingdom which was soon blessed by the rule of Stratocumulus.*

# 35. Forlorn

*I am bit intimidated today, I don't know why?*
*I feel my creation to be without ally...*
*I'm frightened to make friends,*
*because I don't find myself nubiled to take fends.*
*Is this a loneliness please reply*
*but why I'm not lead to deify?*
*Should I inquire what pushes me to this stage,*
*and why I am so disengage?*
*This feeling is so tedium and rampant ,*
*that it has started poisoning me from inside.*
*I endure to be addressed why I am so aberrant?*
*I think I'm no more dignified.*
*Should I sleep, read or wonder?*
*but I feel no more crowded to get an answer.*
*This dullness of mine has affected me a lot ,*
*My friends and family are detached to me in my plot.*
*But I will overcome this drabness and forlorness ,*
*as my positivity is taking me towards joyfullness*
*I am happy that im full of positivity,*
*It is because I never concerned of any passivity.*

# 36. My Father

*He is the eighth wonder of the Earth,*
*He has given me this joyous birth.*
*He has given me all the happiness and mirth,*
*He is none other than my God of this Earth.*
*He has shown infinite love for me,*
*and his expressions always showed a courageous whoopee.*
*I'm blessed to have my dad in my life,*
*and I don't care whosoever criticize.*
*He always encouraged me to be best throughout in my life,*
*and always wanted me to love everyone in bliss of strife.*
*He blessed me with knowledge and abundance of joy,*
*His praises and love cannot be expressed in this envoy.*
*Whenever I need something for my work,*
*He never showed me a dull murk.*
*Inspite of knowing its heavy expenses,*
*he gave me the joy and the happiness withoput any grimaces.*
*He gave me the freedom to go and explore the beauty of the world,*
*knowing the craziness of this netherworld.*
*He gave me the spiritual guidance and knowledge of deeds,*
*so that he can prevent me from misleads.*
*He is a brave person and armour of my body,*
*he is my superstar and my loving and caring DADDY.*
*I thank him for giving me such beautiful powers,*
*as he is my Iron Mna and has all the superpowers.*

# 37. Friends and Friendship

*Friendship is an immortal bond,*
*which has to be donned.*
*To have a healthy relationship between two,*
*it should not be treated as hewe.*
*Friendship has no rule and regulations,*
*it needs no advocation.*
*We are free to make our friends,*
*without following any amends.*
*Friendship is a bond of honour,*
*its body has a thick armour.*
*NO one can break this immortal bond,*
*as it is no more vagabond.*
*Friends are members of family,*
*they are always cordially.*
*These members know our mistakes and weaknesses,*
*and never show their inner grimaces.*
*Friends are never judgemental,*
*and are never apocryphal.*
*They are always with us in our bad situations,*
*without doing any demarcations.*
*This bond needs no sexual verification,*
*it is always pure and should be blessed with no derision.*
*This pious bond is not easily broken,*
*it always makes your beckon.*

*Everyone should have amazing friends,*
*who are with you till your weekends.*

# 38. My Words

*My words speak what I an unable to,*
*they are sometimes short and sometimes long.*
*But they are polite as I am able to make it brie,*
*they are spoken in a host and a throng.*
*My words express me better than my eyes,*
*they tell about me and my pies.*
*People find them creative and incise,*
*but they are without any lies.*
*Words from heart are like petals of rose,*
*in compare to me my words are blossoms which are bestowed.*
*Words from mind are cunning and are like ambrose,*
*In compare to others they are financially bestowed.*
*Words of others are like wallow,*
*they are sometimes meaningful and sometimes hollow.*
*Listen to the words of heart they are always helpful,*
*when you need them they are not deceitful.*

# 39. Mother Earth

*Five billion years ago, a star was formed,*
*with intense heat and pressure it was arrogant of all.*
*It consisted the loops which were showering,*
*ashes and flames around.*
*Can you guess that star is present till now?*
*It was formed by a Bang and a sound,*
*but something unkown was happening all around.*
*Ashes and Smoke were friends of Water,*
*they invited rain to give blessings to their mother.*
*Can you guess that star is present till now?*
*Splattering water all around a small life was found,*
*soon evolution took that life to the 21st Century that is now.*
*Yes, I'm talking about our planet which is a joyful ground,*
*a ground of different ages and different crowns,*
*Yeah, you guessed it right we are living on it now.*
*This star has given us everything,*
*we enjoyed it in abundance and sometimes all.*
*But now everything seems to be on a darker phase,*
*we are surrounded by crisis all around.*
*Yes, it is our Earth who is crying aloud,*
*the day and night we work and run.*
*But can't we take out time to serve the Earth,*
*It's our Mother we all know,*
*we are her children why only she knows?*

*Its our responsibility to revive and help our Mother ,*
*but you are so busy with the other.*
*Today we are under a pandemic ,*
*people say it's a scolding from our Mother.*
*But remember a say : A child can turn into a bad child,*
*but Mother can't be a bad Mother.*
*Now undrstand your responsibilites,*
*bring change all around.*
*She is our Mother who care for us without any bother,*
*show some love to save each other and your Mother.*

# 40. When I am Writing

*When I am writing,*
*Everything in intellect keeps on uprising .*
*When I go ahead writing ,*
*For me it is very inciting .*
*Writing makes me sanguine,*
*This propensity of mine is like a bodkin .*
*It makes my vehemence more intelligible ,*
*For me my writings are like a dextrin .*

# Personal Note

I have been into a lot of situations from my childhood till now and my all experiences have made me so strong that I can even cast a spell on my wordings which is a strange fantasy indeed, but the only one the Father of English Literature William Shakespeare would be proud that I'm now a Social Change Writer. As he truly says, ***"Suit the action to the word, the word to the action."***

*Thanks for reading this book !*

9 798885 219822

Printed by Libri Plureos GmbH in Hamburg,
Germany